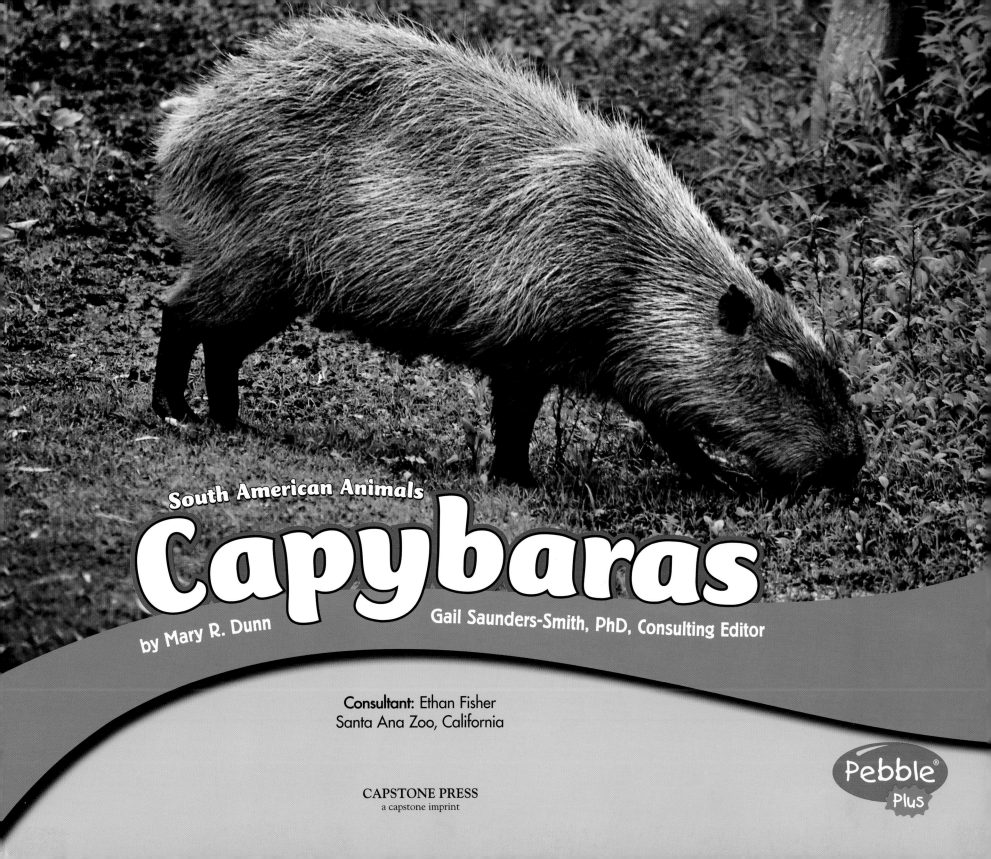

South American Animals

Capybaras

by Mary R. Dunn

Gail Saunders-Smith, PhD, Consulting Editor

Consultant: Ethan Fisher
Santa Ana Zoo, California

Pebble® Plus

CAPSTONE PRESS
a capstone imprint

Pebble Plus is published by Capstone Press,
1710 Roe Crest Drive, North Mankato, Minnesota 56003.
www.capstonepub.com

Library of Congress Cataloging-in-Publication Data
Dunn, Mary R.
    Capybaras / by Mary R. Dunn.
        p. cm.—(Pebble plus. South American animals)
    Includes bibliographical references and index.
    Summary: "Simple text and photographs present capybaras, how they look, where they live,
and what they do"—Provided by publisher.
    ISBN 978-1-4296-8681-5 (library binding)
    ISBN 978-1-62065-322-7 (ebook PDF)
    1. Capybara—Juvenile literature. I. Title.
QL737.R662D86 2013
599.35'9—dc23   2012000297

Editorial Credits
Katy Kudela and Megan Peterson, editors; Gene Bentdahl, designer; Svetlana Zhurkin, photo researcher;
    Kathy McColley, production specialist

Photo Credits
Alamy: F1online digitale Bildagentur, 13, Wildlife, 9; Biosphoto: Luis Casiano, 19; Dreamstime: Lukas Blazek, 17,
Michael Elliott, cover, Ryszard Laskowski, 5; iStockphoto: Lee Torrens, 15; Shutterstock: EcoPrint, 21, E. Sweet, 1,
Richard Peterson, 11, Roberto Tetsuo Okamura, 7

Note to Parents and Teachers

The South American Animals series supports national science standards related to life
science. This book describes and illustrates capybaras. The images support early readers in
understanding the text. The repetition of words and phrases helps early readers learn new
words. This book also introduces early readers to subject-specific vocabulary words, which are
defined in the Glossary section. Early readers may need assistance to read some words and to
use the Table of Contents, Glossary, Read More, Internet Sites, and Index sections of the book.

Printed in the United States of America in North Mankato, Minnesota.
042012   006682CGF12

Table of Contents

Muddy Mammals 4

Up Close! 8

Finding Food 12

Growing Up 14

Staying Safe 18

Glossary 22

Read More 23

Internet Sites 23

Index 24

Muddy Mammals

Splish-splash! Capybaras dive and swim. They roll in mud to keep cool. These mammals are at home in South America's rivers, lakes, and grasslands.

World Map

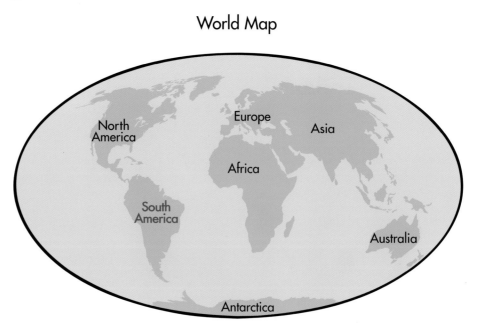

Capybaras roam

Central and South America.

About 10 capybaras

live together

in a family group.

South America Map

where capybaras live

Up Close!

Capybaras are the largest rodents on earth. Adults weigh up to 175 pounds (79 kilograms). They can grow to be more than 4 feet (1.2 meters) long.

Capybaras have large heads

with little eyes and ears.

Their red-brown coats

cover big, round bodies.

Webbed feet help them swim.

webbed feet

Finding Food

With their sharp teeth, capybaras chew on grass. They can eat 8 pounds (3.6 kg) of grass each day. They also munch on water plants.

Growing Up

Female capybaras have one or two litters a year. Each litter has up to eight babies. Females feed milk to their young for about 16 weeks.

After a year, young capybaras leave their family groups.

They start new groups.

In the wild, capybaras live about 10 years.

Staying Safe

Young capybaras move slowly.
They are easy prey
for anacondas. Adults keep
the young safe. They growl
and bark if danger is near.

Jaguars are adult capybaras'
main predator. To stay safe,
capybaras dive underwater.
They hold their breath
for up to five minutes.

Glossary

anaconda—a large, nonpoisonous South American snake that wraps itself tightly around its prey to kill it

jaguar—a large wildcat similar to a leopard, found in the southwestern United States, Mexico, and Central and South America

litter—a group of animals born at the same time to the same mother

mammal—a warm-blooded animal that breathes air; mammals have hair or fur; female mammals feed milk to their young

predator—an animal that hunts other animals for food

prey—an animal hunted by another animal for food

rodent—a mammal with long front teeth used for gnawing; rats, mice, and squirrels are rodents

webbed—having folded skin or tissue between an animal's toes or fingers

Read More

Ganeri, Anita. *Capybara*. A Day in the Life: Rain Forest Animals. Chicago: Heinemann Library, 2011.

Lunis, Natalie. *Capybara: The World's Largest Rodent*. More Supersized! New York: Bearport Pub., 2010.

Salas, Laura Purdie. *Mammals: Hairy, Milk-Making Animals*. Animal Classification. Minneapolis: Picture Window Books, 2010.

Internet Sites

FactHound offers a safe, fun way to find Internet sites related to this book. All of the sites on FactHound have been researched by our staff.

Here's all you do:

Visit *www.facthound.com*

Type in this code: 9781429686815

Index

anacondas, 18

body parts, 10, 12

coats, 10

ears, 10

eating, 12, 14

eyes, 10

families, 6, 16

feet, 10

habitat, 4

jaguars, 20

life span, 16

predators, 18, 20

size, 8, 10

staying safe, 18, 20

swimming, 4, 10, 20

teeth, 12

young, 14, 16, 18

Word Count: 203
Grade: 1
Early-Intervention Level: 16